AUSTRALIA

'Beyond the Black Stump'

Photography by Gary Lewis

List of Contents

Introduction	4-7
Aboriginal Art	8-17
The 'Dreamtime'	18-21
The Aboriginal People	22-29
Aboriginal Children	30-33
'Beyond the Black Stump' – The Outback	34-49
Trees in the Outback	50-57
Water in the Outback	58-69
'The Olgas'	70-71
'Uluru' (Ayers Rock)	72-79
Kakadu and the Wet Regions	80-87
Horses in the Outback	88-91
Cattlemen of the Outback	92-93
Camels in the Outback	94-95
Wildlife in the Dry Regions	96-103
Outback Mining	104-107
People of the 'Bush'	108-113
Favourite Pastimes	114-117
Wildflowers of the Dry Regions	118-121
Bush Homesteads	122-125
Sunsets in the 'Bush'	126-127
Acknowledgements	128

Cover

Hot air balloon, west of Alice Springs, Northern Territory

Title page

Twin ghost gums, Alice Springs, Northern Territory

Left to right

The climbing face, Uluru (Ayers Rock), Northern Territory
Goldmining tower, Kalgoorlie, Western Australia

Introduction

The history of the land we now call Australia has always been one of adaptation to change. Most changes were very gradual, as in the case of the land itself and the plants and animals which first colonised it millions of years ago. Some were more rapid changes, for example the remarkable development of a distinctive Australian vocabulary and accent in the space of a mere two hundred years.

Many English words, such as paddock and creek, assumed entirely different meanings in Australia, and some completely new expressions came into popular useage to cover things beyond the experience of the early English-born settlers.

It quickly became apparent to the early settlers that the interior of Australia was vastly different in terms of climate, topography and scale from the coastal regions where settlement first occurred.

Many uniquely Australian words and phrases were coined to describe the interior, such as the Outback; the Bush; the Backblocks; the Back O'Beyond; the Back O'Bourke (NSW); the Red Centre; the Sunset Country; the Never-Never Country; the Top End; the Overland; and the Dead Heart. Common parlance also had it that when the city dweller went inland he had to travel *down* or *outside*, but when the settler living in the interior travelled to the city he would travel *up* or *inside*.

Beyond the Black Stump is another popular term used to describe the far distant inland regions of Australia. Its origin is obscure although several towns vie for the honour of being the original location of the black stump, notably Coolah in New South Wales, and Mundubbera in Queensland.

Bushman frequently used burnt out trees as landmarks when describing the location of places. Consequently they became local place names, and there would undoubtably have been very many Black Stump creeks, swamps, hills, cattle runs, townships and taverns in the backblocks.

Generally speaking anything described as *Beyond the Black Stump* is so far away as to be almost beyond reckoning, whilst anything *This Side of the Black Stump* is very nearly as far.

Explorers in the early and mid nineteenth century came back from their journeys into the heart of the continent talking in glowing terms of vast grasslands suitable for grazing.

Settlers were quick to take up 'blocks' or 'selections' in these regions. They travelled to them with their wives, families and all their possessions, including large herds of sheep and cattle. Journeys of thousands of miles often took months to complete.

Only the really determined and toughest of families made it to the new lands in the interior and only a few of these stayed on.

They found themselves in the centre of a land so big it could take hours of travelling to meet another human being. It was a dry, dusty country covered in tough desert grasses and with only a few stunted trees for shade. Watercourses and waterholes were few and far between, rainfall was erratic and often non-existent, and above everything the sun blazed unrelentingly.

On the far northern coast the early settlers found a different, but equally harsh climate. Here there was an annual 'wet' season when travelling became totally impossible, and the humidity was almost more insufferable than the heat. In the Gulf area early settlers also found themselves stricken with mysterious fevers.

Apart from townships constructed by the mining companies for their workers, there are few towns of any size in the interior itself. Major centres of population have been restricted to the coastal areas where water is plentiful and the land fertile.

During the thousands of years before Aboriginal man migrated to the continent now called Australia there developed a totally unique range of flora and fauna. The climate then was wetter and cooler and there may have been permanent lakes and waterways in the interior. As the continent drifted south and became totally isolated from Asia the climate changed and the interior of Australia became a hot, arid land. Plants and animals adapted to their changing environment, and there are now many species in Australia which can be found nowhere else in the world.

Plants which grow in the inland areas have to be able to survive with little and irregular supplies of water. In the driest regions there grow mainly grasses, particularly the hardy spinifex, and low growing and spikey-leaved shrubs which survive because they are efficient in storing water and are unpalatable to animals.

Trees are not common and consist mainly of grevilleas, hakeas, wattles and mallees. Although the eucalypt is synonymous with outback Australia, it is rarely found in these dry regions. Occasional stunted specimens are found in chasms, gullies and at the base of rocky outcrops where water is more readily available. Chasms, such as found in the Olgas, often contain remarkably lush vegetation including native palms, and are all the more impressive because of the contrast they form in comparison to the land around them.

Many plants, such as the bottle tree, have developed the ability to store water, a fact utilised by some Aboriginal groups.

Another interesting feature of Australian plant life is the speed with which plants grow, form flowers and seed after rain. Wildflowers bloom in profusion in the desert after rainfall making them one of the scenic delights of the outback.

Australian plant life has developed a resistance to fire as well as drought since this is a common occurrence in the dry regions. Eucalypts, for example, are extremely fire resistant, and in fact many of them produce seeds which require the intensive heat of a bushfire to split them open and allow the seeds to disperse.

The animals of the dry regions have adapted in equally ingenious ways. Many live underground, only venturing out at night when it is cooler to feed. Many can go for great lengths of time without drinking, and some, such as the euro and the rodent mouse, do not need to drink water at all, obtaining all their requirements from the food that they eat.

The breeding cycle of animals in the arid regions is extremely dependant on weather conditions and the amount of food available. Kangaroos, for example, will only bear young if food is plentiful; in periods of drought often going for years at a time without breeding. In good years, however, most of the does will have young in the pouch or will have a very young joey still travelling with them and drinking milk.

Bird life is noticeably more abundant in good seasons. The budgerigar, for example, is capable of breeding at any time of the year and its young reach breeding age only four months after hatching. Populations can therefore increase rapidly when conditions are good.

One of the most amazing stories of adaptation to drought concerns a very special frog which lies 'dormant' under the hard-baked mud of gullies and puddles, often for years at a time until rain falls again. Then, in a race to finish before the water dries up, the frogs mate and produce eggs, which turn into tadpoles and then grow into maturity themselves, all within the space of a few short days.

Aborigines have lived in Australia for at least 40,000 years and perhaps much longer. They are thought to have come across from Asia via the off-shore islands which were then separated only by very narrow stretches of water from Australia.

When they first arrived they lived in the northern coastal areas along the main river systems. The climate was milder then and they would have had no problems finding food and water.

As the climate changed so did the environment, and the Aborigine, along with animals and plants, had to adapt in order to survive.

They learned to live in harmony with the land and its seasons, and the plants and animals which inhabited it. They discovered when fruits and vegetables were safe to eat and when they were poisonous, how to gather them, and which ones had to be cooked to be rendered edible. They learned where to find water, which plants and animals stored drinkable fluids which could be utilised in times of need, and which animals and insects were good to eat and where to find them.

Living close to nature as they did it is hardly surprising that Aborigines should have so many myths and legends to account for the origins of their land and the plant and animal life it contained. These stories constitute the Aboriginal version of the Creation dating back well into 'the mists of time', and are known as the Dreamtime stories.

The Aborigines believe that every feature of the earth, every plant, animal, bird, insect, fish and person was brought into being when a group of Creators, or Ancestral Beings, who acted like humans but looked like birds or animals, travelled across the continent. At every point they rested something was created, and the Aborigines now have a story to describe these events. Aborigines believed that when a woman passed through a certain area Spirit Children floated into her body and she became pregnant. When a baby was born it was therefore a descendant of the animal or bird which visited this area in the Dreamtime.

Thus every Aborigine can trace his existence back to one of the Creators, and those areas of the country his Creator visited. The animal or bird his Creator took the form of also has special significance to him. Abstract symbols represent these totemic Ancestral Beings in art and are restricted in use to certain tribal groups or even to individuals.

Every man, woman and child has, therefore, a direct link with the land he lives on. This close personal link dominates every aspect of the life of the Aborigine. It determines not only the laws they live under and the manner and timing of their ceremonies, but also provides them with a reasonable explanation for everything they see and everything that happens around them.

The coming of the Aborigines has, however, had *some* impact on their environment. They probably brought plants with them, and they certainly brought some animals, most notably the dingo. The extinction of certain species of wildlife can be directly related in time to the coming of the Aborigine and his dog, the dingo. Archaeological evidence proves the existence of the Tasmanian devil and the Tasmanian tiger on the mainland before the dingo was introduced, and significantly the only place where they may be found now is in Tasmania where there are no dingos.

The Aborigine also learned to use fire to his advantage and regularly burned off sections of the bush. This encouraged new growth, drew animals into the area and also minimised the risk to the Aborigines of large uncontrollable fires. Undoubtedly this 'fire-stick' burning must have altered the landscape but to what extent we can only guess.

Unhappily the new English settlers' approaach to the problems he encountered in living and farming in the outback was to try to control and alter his environment. As a result of his efforts there have been noticeable changes in the outback.

Whilst distances are as great as ever, travelling time has been reduced by the building of a network of good roads and railways. Cars, aeroplanes and trains now enable people to travel faster and in greater comfort, and to keep themselves well supplied with all the consumer goods and services they require.

Diesel, wind and solar power generators provide all the power necessary for electrical appliances, such as air-conditioners and refrigerators, which make life more pleasant for the outback family. Whilst the radio is still an important means of communication between people living in the outback, an increasing number now have the use of telephones.

Water is less of a problem now than in the past thanks to our greater knowledge of where to find it and how to control it. Several ambitious schemes have succeeded in diverting, damming and channelling water from areas of regular rainfall to areas where there is little, and as a result many marginal areas are now being intensively farmed.

All this makes life easier for the people who live in the outback, but the basic problems of heat, distance and isolation remain. It has to be concluded then that the reason why so many people live in the outback is because they love it. Statistics prove that an increasing number of people are now choosing to live in the outback and on the northern coasts, perhaps because they like the idea of its hot weather, its wide-open spaces, its fresh air, the stark beauty of its scenery and above all, its uncomplicated life-style.

The superb photographs in this book provide an opportunity to look at that very special part of Australia which is found *Beyond the Black Stump*. It will remind those of us who have had good fortune to visit the outback of the delightfully different flora and fauna to be found there, and bring back memories of the spectacular rugged scenery and the friendliness of its human inhabitants.

For those people who have not yet visited the land *Beyond the Black Stump*, we hope this book will provide the impetus necessary for them to organise a visit very soon.

In the last twenty or more years there has been a resurgence of interest in Aboriginal art, culture and religion, and an appreciation of the way they learned to live *with* their environment rather than trying to control it.

Realisation has dawned for many people that non-Aboriginal Australians have done much harm to their environment. Their greed for material possessions and an easier way of life has led to abuse of the environment and all its natural resources.

Massive areas of Australia have been denuded of trees resulting, in some areas, in severe soil erosion and salinity problems. Recognition of the harmful effects of large-scale land clearing has been slow in coming and measures to counteract these effects, such as re-afforestation, are only now being introduced.

Removal of the forests can have catastrophic effects on the environment, altering as it does the whole balance of nature. Thousands of species of animal and plant life have disappeared forever from this country and introduces species have further added to the unbalancing of the environment.

A more serious consequence of tree clearing, and one which is now being recognised world-wide is, of course, its contribution towards the greenhouse effect and ultimately, therefore, its effect on the world's climate.

There is an increasing awareness amongst Australians of the need for conservation of all our natural resources, and there are many schemes being proposed to try and repair some of the damage done to our land over the last two hundred years.

In line with this, there is a growing appreciation of how very special our country is, and many city-dwellers as well as vast numbers of overseas visitors are now travelling into the outback to view it for themselves.

Aboriginal Art

In a society which lacks a written language art, along with music, dance and story telling, forms an important means of communicating traditions and values.

Aboriginal art is part of a culture stretching back more than 40,000 years. Europeans, with their realistic approach to art did not at first understand the sophistication of ideas behind the Aborigines' seemingly simple and abstract art.

Aboriginal art is primarily religious art, expressing religious beliefs and practices in symbolic form. Most of the designs describe events from the creational period of their past history when in the Dreamtime Ancestral Beings travelled the land forming its main features as they went.

The knowledge to use and interpret these sacred designs is restricted to particular areas, clans and often to individuals. Use of them confirms an individual's relationship to his past, his own particular place in his clan and his attachment to the land where he lives.

Preceding page (left to right)

Aboriginal rock painting, Katherine Gorge, Northern Territory
Aboriginal rock painting, Katherine Gorge, Northern Territory
Aboriginal rock painting, Kakadu, Northern Territory

Above

Aboriginal rock painting, Uluru (Ayers Rock), Northern Territory

Right

Aboriginal rock painting, Kakadu, Northern Territory

Aboriginal Art

The form of expression of Aboriginal art varies considerably from region to region and includes rock painting and carving, sand painting (where the ground is used as the 'canvas' for symbolic designs), decorative design of implements and weapons, and body painting.

Prehistoric art in Australia is almost exclusively rock art since rock was the most durable of the materials used by early Aborigines. However, carved shells, stones and bones possibly up to 15,000 years old have also been found.

Modern rock paintings use the same traditional patterns and designs found in rock paintings dating back thousands of years.

Central Australian art is very abstract but describes the Dreamtime stories and the relationship between man, the land and the plants and animals that inhabit it. Fine examples of these are found at Uluru.

Arnhem Land art is more lively and realistic and contains examples of the famous 'X-ray' style of art which shows internal details of people and animals.

Preceding page
Aboriginal rock painting, Oberi Rock, Kakadu, Northern Territory

Above
Nourlange rock paintings, Northern Territory

Right
N'Dhala Gorge, Northern Territory

Aboriginal Art

Today many of the traditional symbolic designs and drawings found in Aboriginal rock paintings have been modified so that they can be seen publicly. They are painted onto bark, canvas and carved wood, and obtain high prices from tourists and art collectors.

A wide variety of techniques and materials are used but only four basic colours are employed: red, yellow, white and black. The soils and rocks which contain these pigments were once traded between groups from different regions.

The pigments are ground to a paste with water and then mixed with fixatives such as blood, egg, beeswax and orchid juices.

They are applied with brushes made from hair, fibres of palm fronds, feathers and the chewed ends of sticks.

Above

Aboriginal rock painting, Northern Territory

Right

Aboriginal rock painting, Kakadu, Northern Territory

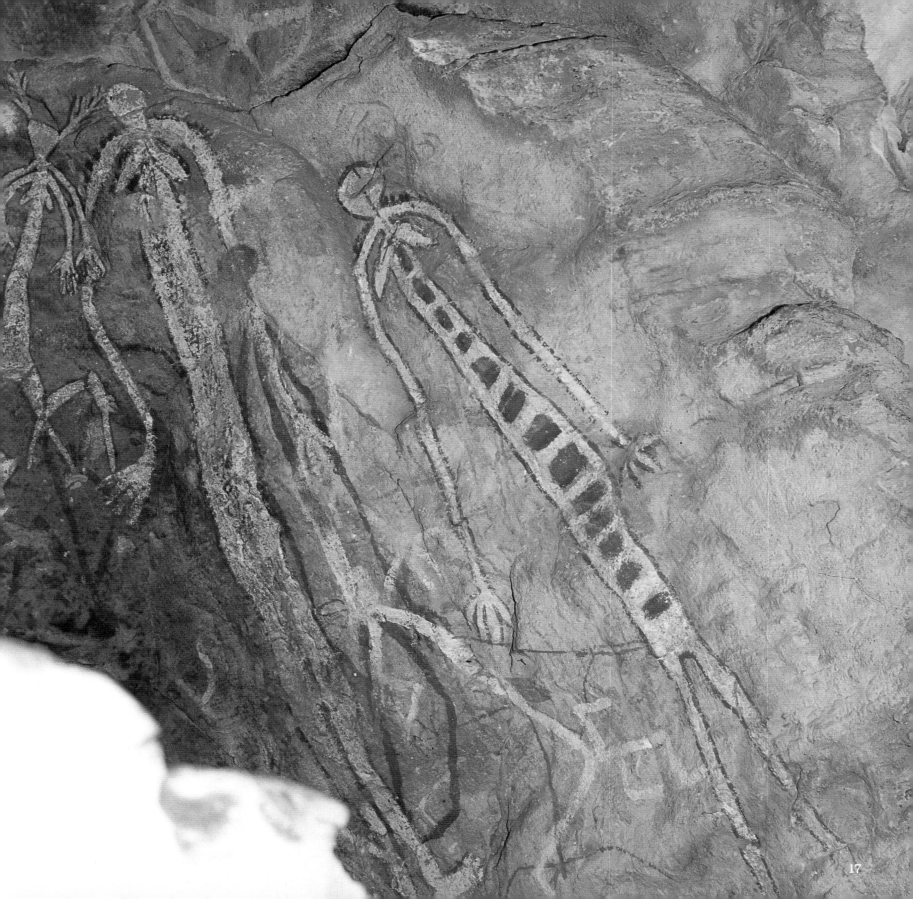

Aboriginal Dreamtime

The *Dreamtime* is a collection of information passed on from one generation to another in a stylised and basically oral form, which provides Aborigines with an explanation of the creation of their land and also expresses the fundamental relationship between them and their environment.

In the beginning the land was flat and bare. Ancestral Beings, or Creators, roamed the earth, and Dreamtime stories relate how in their travels they formed all the topographical features, and the people, plants and animals as they exist today.

For the Aborigine, relating or re-enacting the Dreamtime stories brings him into direct spiritual communion with his ancestors, and re-affirms his very being.

Many Aborigines today still live their lives following the dictates of their individual Dreaming. One way this is done is through song and dance cycles which may take days or weeks to perform, and which have been passed on in this manner for thousands of years.

Preceding page
Aboriginal 'Dreamtime' display, Alice Springs, Northern Territory
Above and right
Aboriginal 'Dreamtime' display, Alice Springs, Northern Territory

Aboriginal People

Archaeological evidence suggests that Aborigines have inhabited the Australian continent for at least 40,000 years, having arrived from Asia by canoe or raft when the sea channel between its offshore islands and Australia was much narrower than now.

From about 300,000 people in 1788, numbers of Aborigines declined rapidly at first due to persecution, disease and starvation, but in recent years appears to have increased reaching about 228,000 in 1986.

Quite a significant number of these now live in the large cities, living a western style of life. Others live as fringe dwellers around towns and smaller cities, predominantly in the north of the country.

An increasing number are electing to live in a traditional manner in the bush, although few can claim to live a lifestyle totally uninfluenced by western 'civilisation'

Preceding page

Aboriginal artefacts, Alice Springs, Northern Territory

Above

Aboriginal woman basket-weaving, far-north Quensland

Right

Mia Mia, Aboriginal bark hut, far-north Queensland

Aboriginal People

Aborigines live in extended family groupings which have closely defined and intricate systems of relationships, rights and obligations.

Several families may live together as a 'band' within a larger group who share a common language and 'Dreaming', and who join together from time to time for ceremonial purposes. These bands live together, hunting and gathering food within a geographic area determined by totemic Ancestral Beings from the Dreamtime from whom band members claim descent.

Traditionally Aborigines wore little or no clothing, building slow burning, smokey fires in the centre of a shelter constructed from brush and bark to protect them from the cold and mosquitoes. Caves were used as temporary residences during heavy rain.

Weapons and implements were built from stone, wood and bone. Aborigines had no knowledge of metals prior to the white man's arrival.

Preceding page (left to right)

Traditional Aboriginal hunter, Kakadu, Northern Territory
Aboriginal, Uluru (Ayers Rock), Northern Territory
Traditional Aboriginal hunter, Kakadu, Northern Territory

Above

Thursday Island Aboriginal, far-north Queensland

Right

Traditional Aboriginal dance, Melville Island,

Aboriginal Children

Traditionally Aboriginal children were brought up as part of an extended social group, surrounded by security and affection, and with a natural acceptance and understanding of their role and purpose in life.

Their highly structured system of living was shattered by the intrusion of the white man who did not appreciate the sophistication behind their simple stone-age way of life.

Until relatively recently Aboriginal children were often taken away from their parents and sent to Mission schools to be 'educated'. Many were then put into service and never saw their families again.

There is nowadays a mounting awareness amongst Aborigines of the need to restore the old family structures and codes of living and thereby to return a sense of self-esteem and dignity to the Aboriginal people. Many Aboriginal children are now being taught their traditional languages, customs and traditions in school alongside the modern curriculum.

Preceding page (left to right)

Aboriginal children, Jay Creek, Alice Springs, Northern Territory
Alice Springs School
Young Aboriginal, Kakadu, Northern Territory

Above

Young Aboriginal children, Alice Springs rodeo, Northern Territory

Right

Aboriginal school children, Alice Springs, Northern Territory

'Beyond the Black Stump'

With an average for the whole of Australia of only 1.6 persons per square kilometre and more than 65% of the total population living in the capital cities, the interior of the continent must be considered a very sparsely populated region.

The people of the interior are isolated by geographic and climatic factors from the main centres of population, and many outback communities still lack good all-weather roads or reliable communications with the outside world.

Distances between places are so vast that many farmers use aeroplanes as well as cars for travelling, and the two-way radio is still the main form of communciation with others.

There are few schools in the outback so children are educated via the famous 'School of the Air'. The Royal Flying Doctor Service provides emergency medical aid to isolated communities.

Prceding page

Outback gorge, north-west Western Australia

Above

Corroboree Rock, east of Alice Springs, Northern Territory

Right

Typical outback vegetation, west of Alice Springs, Northern Territory

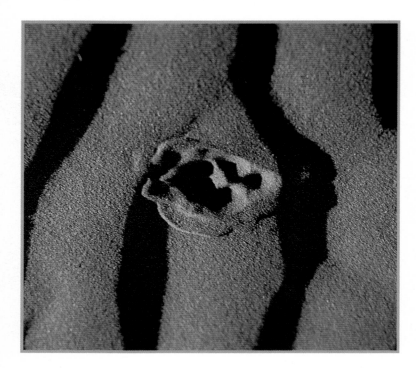

'Beyond the Black Stump'

Australia's history is so recent that the interior has only really in the last twenty years been properly mapped and explored.

Major expeditions in the early and mid-nineteenth century established most of the main geographical features of the continent in the face of incredible hardship and trials of endurance.

The rough terrain and arid nature of the interior made travelling extremely difficult, and it was nearly 100 years before the continent was crossed from south to north. Over the next fifty years most of the rest of Australia was explored and mapped. Brave and resourceful pioneers soon followed the explorers into the interior and established farms and cattle and sheep stations.

Many features in central Australia were named in honour of these early explorers and pioneers.

Preceding page (left to right)

King's Canyon, Northern Territory
King's Canyon, Northern Territory
Termite hill, Wittenoom Gorge, north-west Western Australia

Above

Animal tracks, red sand, Simpson Desert, Northern Territory

Right

Historic marker, Ayer Highway, Northern Territory

'Beyond the Black Stump'

Australia's climate is one of extremes, from mild temperatures and regular rainfall in the south to heavy rainfall and consistently high temperatures in the tropical north east.

In the interior great extremes of temperature are experienced. In winter temperatures may fall at night to freezing, and rise to 20 degrees Celsius or more during the day, and in summer long periods of intense heat are regularly recorded for weeks at a stretch in the north-west of the country.

Rainfall is erratic with some areas experiencing drought for years at a time. When rain does fall it is usually very heavy and has an extremely errosive effect on the landscape. It also causes the dormant plant life to awaken and grow lush and green, and the wildflowers to bloom.

Preceding page

Flinders Ranges, South Australia

Above

Sunset over cane country, far-north Queensland

Right

Sunset over poppet-head, Kalgoorlie, Western Australia

'Beyond the Black Stump'

In geological terms Australia is an ancient land. Its geological history can be traced back over a period of 3,000 million years.

The ancient rocks that form the continent are mostly overlaid by more recent sedimentary deposits, but are exposed in some areas as hills, monoliths and other striking rock formations.

Most of central Austalia has little surface water due to the low and erratic rainfall, but underneath much of the land is a vast lake of water, known as the Great Artesian Basin, which can be tapped to provide water for people and stock.

Preceding page

Standley Chasm, west of Alice Springs, Northern Territory

Above

Macdonnnell Ranges, west of Alice Springs, Northern Territory

Right

Mt. Tom Price, far-north Western Australia

Trees in the Outback

The Australian landscape is dominated by eucalypts, more popularly known as gum trees, of which over 500 species have been distinguished.

Eucalypts are not common in arid regions with only a few stunted specimens, mostly red gums and ghost gums, being found in watercourses and gorges. The most commonly found trees are wattles, coolabahs, mallees and hakeas, none of which grow to a great height.

However, the magnificient eucalypt with its fragrant, smooth-edged, grey-green leaves is synonymous with outback Australia. In a hot dry climate where little grows, trees are a welcome source of shade to animals and man alike. The majestic eucalypt also forms a very distinctive landmark in what is often otherwise a featureless landscape.

Preceding page

The Olgas, Northern Territory
Standley Chasm, west of Alice Springs, Northern Territory
Near Trephina Gorge, Northern Territory

Above

In the 'Old Telegraph Station', Alice Springs, Northern Territory

Right

Iron-ore country, north-west Western Australia

Trees in the Outback

Eucalypts have a wonderful ability to adapt themselves to their own particular environment.

In very arid areas eucalypts have fine needle-like leaves to minimise water loss, whilst in wetter areas other characteristics have evolved. In remote Alpine regions where conditions are also very harsh the snow gum has specially adapted to be able to survive long periods of intense cold.

Eucalypts have a special relationship with fire. They have the ability to survive high temperatures, and fire is often necessary to burst open seed pods to assist in the regeneration of the species.

Preceding page (left to right)

Mt. Wellington, Tasmania
Ross River, Northern Territory
Standley Chasm, west of Alice Springs, Northern Territory

Above

Near Trephina Gorge, Northern Territory

Right

In the 'Old Telegraph Station', Alice Springs, Northern Territory

Water in the Outback

Water is often considered to be Australia's most valuable resource, and in central Australia where surface water is very scarce this is undoubtedly true. Rainfall is low and erratic and temperatures and evaporation rates are high.

Watercourses have been diverted and channelled in some regions to provide water for irrigated farming. However, in vast stretches of the interior there is no permanent surface water and water has to be obtained from deep bores which tap the artesian water supplies. In times of prolonged drought even these bores may dry up and stock losses may be severe.

Preceding page
Todd River sunrise, Alice Springs, Northern Territory

Above
Emily Gap, east of Alice Springs, Northern Territory

Right
Palm Valley, Northern Territory

Water in the Outback

Permanent watercourses are basically confined to the northern coastal regions where monsoonal rain occurs each summer to replenish supplies.

Watercourses in the interior are usually dry for most of the year, turning into raging torrents in just a few hours after a heavy downpour of rain.

When rain does fall in the outback, it is usually very heavy and can cause great damage to the environment. Once the floods have subsided a little however, wildflowers and grasses grow in lush profusion and soon obliterate the scarring of the floodwaters.

Preceding page (left to right)

Outback gorge, north-west Western Australia
Red Gorge, north-west Western Australia
Red Gorge, north-west Western Australia

Above

Water course, north-west Western Australia

Right

Todd River, Alice Springs, Northern Territory

Water in the Outback

Permanent surface water in the outback is rare and mainly found in gullies and chasms where water collects in deep holes in the rocks. Around these waterholes can be found plenty of evidence of the centuries of Aboriginal useage; rock paintings and rock carvings are often found together with the more recent evidence of campfire ashes.

Waterholes have a special significance to Aborigines as proof of the authenticity of ancient Dreamtime stories, when Creators travelled across the country creating all the natural features as they went.

For the early explorers and settlers finding these sources of water was of critical importance as their very survival depended on them. Aborigines often befriended explorers and settlers and showed them where to find water.

Preceding page (left to right)
Jessie Gap, Northern Territory
Simpson's Gap, Northern Territory
Water course, Trephina Gorge, Northern Territory
Above
Emily Gap, east of Alice Springs, Northern Territory
Right
King's Canyon, Northern Territory

'The Olgas'

The Olgas are a spectacular group of giant, brilliant red monoliths located about 350 kilometres from Alice Springs, and are part of the Uluru National Park.

The largest of the monoliths rises 450 metres above the surrounding plains. Clustered around it are nearly 30 lesser rocks, and between them run deep gorges which support an incredible range of wildlife and lush tropical vegetation. Understandably, they are a very popular tourist destination.

The Olgas are called *Katatjuta* by their local Aboriginal owners and have great religious significance for them.

Ancient rock carvings are found amongst them and numerous Dreamtime legends are associated with individual rock features.

Above and right
The Olgas, Northern Territory

'Uluru'

Uluru, about 450 kilometres south-west of Alice Springs, is the largest single rock or monolith in the world, and as part of the Uluru National Park was deemed of such world significance that it received World Heritage Listing in 1987.

Standing over 335 metres above an open windswept plain the monolith is 8.8 kilometres in circumference.

Busloads of tourists come each year to enjoy the spectacular changes in the colour of the rock at different times of day, and also the wonderful views from the summit.

The sides of the monolith are scarred by gullies which become transformed into thundering 250 metre waterfalls after heavy rain.

Preceding page

The climbing face, early morning, Uluru (Ayers Rock), Northern Territory

Above and right

Coach tours, Uluru (Ayers Rock), Northern Territory

'Uluru'

Uluru is the Aboriginal name for what was once called Ayers Rock.

In 1985 inalienable freehold title to the Uluru National Park was given to the Matijula Aboriginal Community in recognition of its extreme significance to them.

The rock is held sacred by Aborigines who associate it with many legends of the Dreamtime. Gullies, ridges, caves and rock holes in its surface, and soaks at its base all have particular significance to them.

An important Creation serpent-snake legend concerns one of its rock holes, and many of the overhangs and caves are covered in rock carvings and paintings of great antiquity and beauty.

Preceding page (left to right)
The Kangaroo Tail, Uluru (Ayers Rock), Northern Territory
The climbing face, Uluru (Ayers Rock), Northern Territory
Rockface and boulders, Uluru (Ayers Rock), Northern Territory
Above and right
Uluru (Ayers Rock), Northern Territory

Kakadu and the Wetlands

Kakadu National Park covers a large part of Arnhem Land and has been awarded World Heritage Listing for its unique, virtually untouched wetlands and upland forests.

An escarpment 450 metres high dominates the park. At its base is one of the world's greatest collections of cave paintings, dating back over 18,000 years.

Controversy continues about allowing mining within the park boundaries because of its destructive effect on the environment. Currently uranium mining occurs near Jabiru, and other sites are still being considered.

Wild horses and water buffalo introduced earlier to Kakadu cause considerable damage to the park and are now being systematically removed by the rangers.

Preceding page

Outback grasses

Above and right

Water buffalo, Kakadu, Northern Territory

Kakadu & the Wetlands

Kakadu National Park includes dry upland forests and grasslands and also floodplains inundated each year during the wet season. The range of flora and fauna is extraordinarily diverse and includes 270 species of birds, 50 native mammals, and over 1,000 plant species.

Lagoons and waterways become a dry season haven for millions of birds and other wildlife. The thousands of water birds that congregate at dusk in the wetlands are a spectacular sight, and the park is much favoured by tourists.

The estuaries and rivers are also the home of salt and freshwater crocodiles and the giant barramundi.

Preceding page (left to right)

Rainbow birds, Kakadu, Northern Territory
Rainbow birds, Kakadu, Northern Territory
Black Kites, Kakadu, Northern Territory

Above

Jabirus, Kakadu, Northern Territory

Right

Pied Heron, Kakadu, Northern Territory

Horses in the Outback

Although wild horses, or brumbies, roam much of inland Australia they are not native to this country.

Horses arrived with the First Fleet, and in regular shipments thereafter, for use in farming and for carriage and saddle work. Without them exploration of the continent would have been almost impossible.

Although the car, aeroplane, helicopter and tractor have taken over much of the horse's work it is still considered to be indispensable to cattlemen.

Brumbies are descended from horses which strayed or were deliberately released. They roam large parts of the high country and inland areas in large bands, and have achieved plague proportions in some areas. They are thought to cause much damage to property and are often culled.

Preceding page

Brumby round-up, Ross River, Northern Territory

Above

Jackeroo, Ross River, Northern Territory

Right

Water crossing, Ross River, Northern Territory

Cattlemen of the Outback

Once the route to the interior had been explored sheep and cattle began to be 'overlanded', or herded, large distances to stock new stations.

Drovers would take large herds thousands of miles across inhospitable country, journeys often taking months or even years.

Cattle and sheep were also overlanded along recognised stock routes, such as the Birdsville Track, to railheads or country markets.

Since the 1950's the use of road-trains and railways, and an increase in the number of meatworks in northern Australia has reduced the need for overlanding of stock.

Droving will, however, always be necessary in remote areas where roads are unsuitable for heavy vehicles, and although helicopters and motorcycles are used in mustering cattle, the horse will never be entirely replaced for general station work.

Above and right

Cattleman of the Outback, Glen Helen, Northern Territory

Camels in the Outback

In a strange twist of circumstances Australia has recently begun exporting camels to Arabia. Camels, shipped here first in 1860 for the Burke and Wills expedition and subsequently imported for use as work animals, have flourished in Australia and are in great demand throughout the world.

From 1865 camels were imported for use in exploration, and generally for carrying supplies, people and produce. They continued in this use until the early 1900's when the car, aeroplane and railway began to take over their work.

They are little used in general station work now but are experiencing a revival in popularity for outback trekking.

About 25,000 wild camels now roam inland Australia. In some areas they are considered pests and regularly culled.

Above and right
Camel safaris, Alice Springs, Northern Territory

Wildlife of the Dry Regions

Three-quarters of the Australian mainland can be classified as arid, but its interior supports an abundance of plant and animal life.

Many of these animals live most of their lives below ground out of the harsh sun, and some of the larger mammals and birds have adapted in unusual ways to their changing environment. Kangaroos, for example, stop breeding in times of drought to reduce pressure on food supplies, and some species can exist without drinking water.

All animal and bird populations vary according to the food and water available, but even in the worst of droughts life endures.

Preceding page (left to right)

Dingo — Sand Goanna — Emu

Above

King Brown Snake

Right

Brown Tree Snake

Wildlife of the Dry Regions

Light rainfall can have a significant effect on the bush, but when heavy rain falls it dramatically alters the landscape, causing creeks to flood and lakes to form.

Bird, animal and plant life all flourish under these conditions. Grasses grow lush and green, and colourful wildflowers transform the otherwise drab country into a scene of great beauty.

Cockatoos, galahs, budgerigars and waterbirds all breed prolifically when conditions are good, and their wheeling flocks make an unforgettable sight.

Trees, such as eucalypts and mallees, with their deep root systems can also survive long periods of drought to flourish and flower in good seasons.

Preceding page

Red Kangaroo, Northern Territory

Above

Butcher Bird

Right

Bustard or Plains Turkey

Outback Mining

Mt. Tom Price is one of several large high-grade iron ore deposits being mined in the Hamersley Range of north-western Australia. Ore quarried from the opencut mine is carried by rail 295 kilometres to the port of Dampier and shipped, mainly overseas, for processing.

Mining here is carried out on a massive, capital intensive scale using the best quarrying, earth-moving and ore carrying equipment available.

The township of Tom Price, constructed when the mine opened in 1964, is typical of mining towns in the region. Developed privately by Hamersley Iron Pty.Ltd., it provides everything its miners and their families could possibly need.

Preceding page

Iron-ore mining, Mt. Tom Price, north-west Western Australia

Above and right

Iron-ore mining, Mt. Tom Price, north-west Western Australia

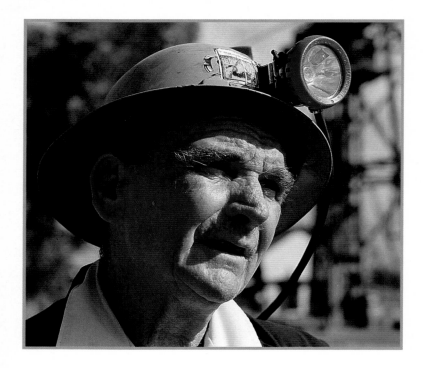

People of the 'Bush'

Australia's remote regions are populated by a diverse range of people all with one thing in common: their love of the outback.

For its Aboriginal inhabitants with their simple life-style, and knowing no other climate or landscape, the outback is their home and they are happy living there. But for non-Aboriginal Australians there has to be some other reason for them to stay there. They live separated by hundreds and sometimes thousands of kilometres from what can often only loosely be called 'civilisation'. The climate is harsh and often unforgiving, and they have very few of the facilities that city-dwellers take so much for granted.

Preceding page

Afternoon silhouettes, Alice Springs rodeo, Northern Territory

Above

Gold-miner, Kalgoorlie, Western Australia

Right

'Lofty', Ayers Rock tour guide, Northern Territory

People of the 'Bush'

The wide open spaces, the stark grandeur of its mountains and valleys, and the brilliant and changing colours of the bush in its different seasons, are all attractions to outback dwellers. Many people prefer the outback's uncomplicated life-style and clean air. Above all there is the quality of 'mate-ship' which in remote areas is a very special bond between people helping them overcome feelings of loneliness and deprivation.

Increasing tourism in the remote areas of Australia means that prospecting, mining and station work are not the only sources of income. Now people work as tour guides, run wildlife parks and pioneer museums, work in hotels and restaurants, make and sell art and craftwork.

Above

Proprietor, 'The Old Lolly Shop', Swan Hill, Victoria

Right

James Egan, Outback artist

Pastimes (Horse Racing)

To the people of the bush social contact with others through events such as race meetings, rodeos and country shows, is vitally important in helping combat the loneliness and deprivation of their lifestyle.

The horse has always been so central to the lives of outback dwellers it is hardly surprising that many of their forms of entertainment also revolve around the horse.

Country towns of any decent size boast their own racecourse, varying in standard from dusty tracks to well kept turf courses, but all are well patronised on racedays. The annual Birdsville races have become a popular event not only for locals, but also for visitors from the cities and overseas tourists.

Camels have in recent times become the subject of an upsurge in public interest, and camel races are now regular events in outback towns.

Above and right

Outback horse-racing, Darwin, Northern Territory

Pastimes (Rodeos)

Rodeos had their beginnings in local bush shows where
cattlemen could display their skills in horse riding and cattle
handling. Since 1945 when the first Australian
Championships were held, these informal competitions have
developed into the rodeo circuit as we now know it. It has a
set of rules and standards laid down by a governing body,
and high prize money is now being offered to contestants.

Rodeos are an exciting and colourful spectacle and
attract large crowds wherever they are held. Events include
buckjumping (bronco-riding), steer wrestling (bulldogging),
and roping. Some contestants make a living from following
the rodeo circuit.

Above

Bull riding, Outback rodeo

Right

Alice Springs rodeo, Northern Territory

Wildflowers of the Dry Regions

The isolation of the Australian continent for tens of millions of years led to the evolution of a range of flora and fauna quite without parallel in the world.

Australia's best wildflower displays are seen in the more arid regions such as parts of south-western Australia, the Flinders Ranges in South Australia and the 'Red Centre' itself. These areas have mainly been incorporated into National Parks, and are visited and much admired by thousands of tourists each year.

Most of Australia's wildflowers are native to Australia but several introduced species, most notably the infamous 'Paterson's Curse', have flourished here and now rival the native wildflowers in their scenic splendour.

Many wildflowers are now being cultivated for suburban gardens, and there is a small but growing export market in cut, dried, Australian wildflowers.

Preceding page (left to right)
Sturt's Desert Pea — Cottontails — Wattle, Northern Territory
Above
Desert Grevillea, Uluru (Ayers Rock), Northern Territory
Right
Mulla-Mulla, north-west Western Australia

Bush Homesteads

One of the most interesting of the European settlers' adaptations to living conditions in central Australia has been the development of a distinctive style of housing, the bush homestead.

The typical bush homestead was a single storied structure raised on stilts to catch cooling breezes, with a corrugated iron roof and a broad verandah shading all four sides.

Modern bush homesteads retain all the traditional features with a few added 'extras'. Television and telephone are now available to inland areas, and diesel generators supply power for air conditioners, refrigerators and electric lights. Outbuildings contain tools and spare parts to keep the station's modern mechanical equipment functioning, and a helicopter or light aeroplane may be parked close by.

But the heat, the dust and the flies remain the same, making the homestead the haven it always has been for the hardworking outback cattleman.

Above

Outback homestead, Queensland-Northern Territory border

Right

Ross River homestead, Northern Territory

Bush Homesteads

In pioneering days settlers arrived from England with little other than enthusiasm to help them come to terms with farming under Australian conditions.

The rainfall in many areas of the inland proved over a period of years to be inadequate for farming, and many families were forced to abandon their properties and return to the cities to earn a living.

Their houses, stripped of their more useful building materials, soon returned to the bush with only the stone chimneys to prove that they were ever there. More recently deserted houses may have their walls and roof basically intact, but the bush will already have started to take over.

The marginal areas of Australia's wheat belt contain many such sad reminders of unsuccessful farming ventures.

Above

Outback 'dunny'

Right

Deserted homestead

Sunsets in the 'Bush'

After a fascinating and maybe arduous day's travel in the outback there is no more fitting ending than watching the sun go down, colouring with its dying rays the dramatic scenery of the mountains or the desert.

Every evening hundreds of tourists wait with cameras poised to capture Uluru (Ayers Rock) which at sunset becomes a deep ruby red colour: a much photographed scene but still an unforgettable experience for all those present.

Equally as beautiful and no less Australian are those scenes which show the sun setting behind homesteads, tank stands and windmills. These pictures encapsulate the very essence of the Australian outback, with the red glow of the setting sun providing a rich backdrop for the very symbols of man's attempt to control his environment - his dwelling place and his means of obtaining water.

Above and right

Sunset over wind vane and tanks, Northern Territory

Acknowledgements

First published in Australia in 1990 by:

Peter Antill-Rose and Associates Pty Ltd
63 Kingsway
Glen Waverley
Victoria 3150
Australia

Telephone (03) 562 0221
Facsimile (03) 562 0190

Photographs by Gary Lewis
Pictorial editing by Allan Cornwell

Designed by Small Back Room Productions, Upwey, Victoria
Typeset by Paragraphics, Ferntree Gully, Victoria
Produced in Hong Kong by Mandarin Offset

ISBN 1 86282 045 7

Right

Kakadu sunset, Northern Territory